EXPLORING OUR RAINFOREST

HARPY EAGLE

SUSAN H. GRAY

Published in the United States of America by Cherry Lake Publishing
Ann Arbor, Michigan
www.cherrylakepublishing.com

Content Adviser: Dr. Stephen S. Ditchkoff, Professor of Wildlife Ecology, Auburn University, Alabama
Reading Adviser: Marla Conn, ReadAbility, Inc.

Photo Credits: ©MarcusVDT/Shutterstock Images, cover, 1, 9; ©Batman2000/CanStockPhoto, 5; ©BirdLife International and NatureServe (2014) Bird Species Distribution Maps of the World. 2013, 6; ©worldswildlifewonders/Shutterstock Images, 7; ©Kenneth Lilly/Thinkstock, 10; ©Reisbegeleidercom/iStock, 11; ©Alfredo Maiquez/Shutterstock Images, 12; ©Paul Spurling/The Peregrine Fund, 13; ©nattanan726/Shutterstock Images, 15; ©kirsten/http://www.flickr.com/CC-BY-SA 2.0, 16; ©David Morimoto/http://www.flickr.com/CC-BY-SA 2.0, 19; ©FLAVIOCONCEICAOFOTOS/iStock, 21; ©Mark Jones/Media Bakery, 22; ©TakinPix/iStock, 25; ©NTCo/iStock, 27; ©Ron Knight/http://www.flickr.com/CC-BY-2.0, 29

Library of Congress Cataloging-in-Publication Data

Gray, Susan Heinrichs, author.
Harpy eagle / Susan H. Gray.
    pages cm. — (Exploring our rainforests)
  Summary: "Introduces facts about harpy eagles, including physical features, habitat, life cycle, food, and threats to these rainforest creatures. Photos, captions, and keywords supplement the narrative of this informational text."
— Provided by publisher.
  Audience: Ages 8-12.
  Audience: Grades 4 to 6.
  Includes bibliographical references and index.
  ISBN 978-1-63188-976-9 (hardcover) — ISBN 978-1-63362-015-5 (pbk.) — ISBN 978-1-63362-054-4 (pdf)
  — ISBN 978-1-63362-093-3 (ebook) 1. Harpy eagle—Juvenile literature. 2. Eagles—Juvenile literature. I. Title.

  QL696.F32G74 2014
  598.9'42—dc23   2014020996

Cherry Lake Publishing would like to acknowledge the work of
The Partnership for 21st Century Skills. Please visit www.p21.org
for more information.

Printed in the United States of America
Corporate Graphics

ABOUT THE AUTHOR

Susan H. Gray has a master's degree in zoology. She has worked in research and has taught college-level science classes. Susan has also written more than 140 science and reference books, but especially likes to write about animals. She and her husband, Michael, live in Cabot, Arkansas.

TABLE OF CONTENTS

A Lizard for Lunch

Whoosh! High up in the treetops, the harpy eagle swoops through the leaves and lands on a branch. As he lands, his head and tail bob to keep his body balanced. Once he is steady, he folds his wings against his body. He adjusts his feet a little until he feels comfortable.

The eagle stands and looks down into the forest. He sees the tangle of tree trunks, roots, and vines. He hears the monkeys barking and howling. He senses the warm, damp air all about him. He stands. And he stands. Hours pass.

Suddenly, he sees it—the perfect meal! Far below him,

a large lizard is creeping along a branch. The eagle dives toward the reptile, using his tail to steer right to it. He adjusts his wings to slow his descent.

In one quick move, the eagle snags the lizard and swoops upward. Then he heads to his nest. This lizard will make a great meal for his mate.

Harpy eagles are fierce hunters.

RANGE MAP

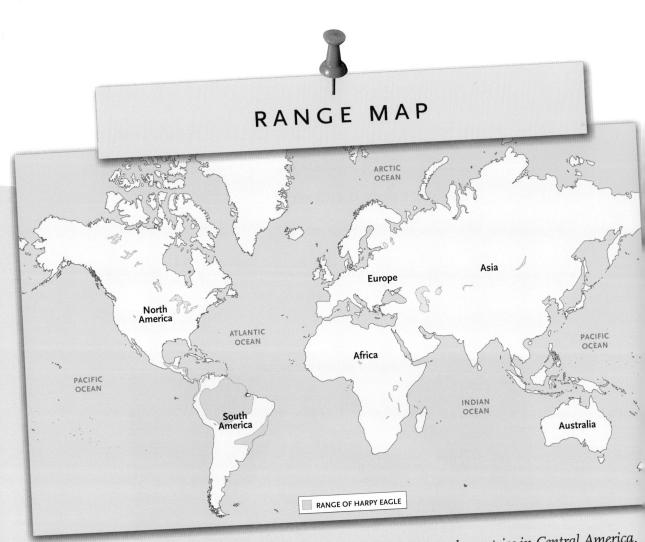

RANGE OF HARPY EAGLE

Harpy eagles live in a broad area of South America, as in well as several countries in Central America.

Harpy eagles live in the rainforests of South America, Central America, and Mexico. They prefer to stay within the forest **canopy**, where they hunt, eat, build nests, mate, and raise their young.

In ancient Greek myths, a harpy is a creature with the body of a bird and the face of a woman. These harpies never actually existed. But when a scientist named Carl Linnaeus first saw the eagles in the 1700s, he thought they had intense, feminine faces. He named them after the harpies of Greek legends.

The harpy eagle has distinct feathers around its face.

LOOK AGAIN

LINNAEUS SAW HARPY FACES JUST LIKE THIS ONE. WHICH FEATURES MADE IT LOOK HUMAN TO HIM?

A Bird Built for Hunting

The harpy eagle is an **apex** predator. An apex predator is an animal with no natural enemies. It lives by hunting and eating other animals. But no other animal hunts it.

Harpies are among the largest birds in the world. Males can weigh up to 12 pounds (5.4 kilograms). Females, however, can weigh as much as 20 pounds (9 kg). This is 100 times the weight of a robin!

This handsome eagle has black feathers on its back and white ones on its belly. Gray feathers cover its face.

The wings and tail have alternating bands of black and white.

Many of the bird's features make it an outstanding hunter. Its vision is excellent. The eagle can spy something smaller than a mouse from 220 yards (201 meters) away.

Harpy eagles have outstanding vision, which lets them spot their prey from a very long distance.

BODY DIAGRAM

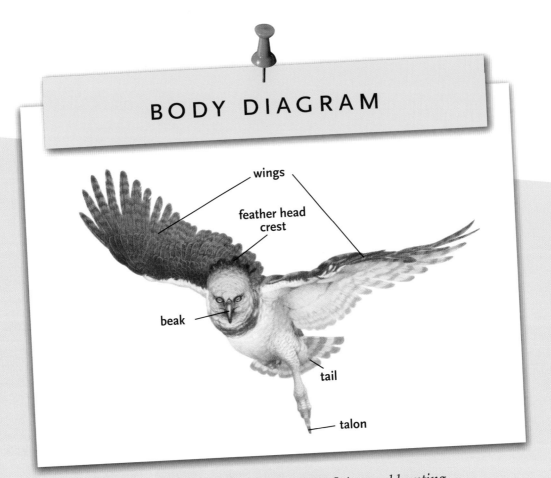

wings

feather head
crest

beak

tail

talon

Harpy eagles have bodies designed for flying and hunting.

Feathers on the harpy's face form a disk, similar to the face of an owl. The eagle can raise these disk feathers, which may aid its hearing by directing sounds toward the ears. Crowning the head are several long feathers. The bird raises these when it's alarmed.

Harpy eagles have sharp, powerful beaks.

The eagle's strong neck and sharp beak are ideal for eating meat. These two features enable the harpy to tear its prey apart. Bird experts who have watched these predators feed report that the bird will strip the skin right off its dead prey.

The harpy's chest, back, and shoulder muscles are very strong. These muscles power the wings, and strong wings are required to move such a huge eagle through the air.

The talons of a harpy eagle are useful for hunting and for holding onto tree branches.

The harpy's large tail can twist, turn, and spread out like a fan. This helps the eagle maneuver through the trees. A bird that spends its time in the canopy must be able to make quick turns, change direction easily, and dodge tree limbs. The tail makes all of this possible.

The legs and feet are also those of a mighty hunter. The legs are thick and strong. Each foot has four toes—three in front and one in back. Each toe ends in a huge **talon**. The talons are curved, sharp, and up to 5 inches (12.7 centimeters) in length.

People who work with harpy eagles need to wear protective gloves.

LOOK AGAIN

THIS HARPY EAGLE IS ABOUT TO LAND. WHAT IS ITS
BODY DOING TO PREPARE FOR A LANDING?

FOOD IN THE FOREST

Harpy eagles eat a variety of rainforest animals. Their prey includes reptiles such as snakes and iguanas. They also feed on other birds, including parrots and macaws. **Mammals** make up most of their diet, though. Harpy eagles are known to eat foxes, monkeys, young deer, opossums, anteaters, and **peccaries**. They also chow down on porcupines. Somehow, the porcupine quills do not bother them.

The sloth is one of the eagle's favorite foods. Sloths hang horizontally below tree branches. They travel at an incredibly slow pace. The slow movement usually makes sloths easy targets for harpies. But the sloth does have one defense. It has very long claws and knows how to use them. When threatened, the sloth can slash out with remarkable speed. Young harpies with little hunting experience learn quickly to avoid the sloth's claws.

Because sloths move so slowly, harpy eagles have an easy time catching them.

The eagle does not hunt by soaring above the canopy. Instead, it takes short flights from tree to tree. It may also perch on a branch, staring into the forest for hours. All the while, it counts on its sharp vision and hearing to detect prey.

When the harpy spots its victim, it swoops in and kills it quickly. Eagles may begin eating unusually large prey right on the spot. Or they may drag it to a higher place to be devoured. Once the prey has been eaten down to a smaller size, the harpy may haul it back to the nest. This is when those powerful wing muscles come in handy.

Harpies can take days to eat an animal. All that time, the

This harpy eagle has caught a howler monkey.

[21ST CENTURY SKILLS LIBRARY]

meat sits out in the hot and humid rainforest. It becomes rotten and stinky. Such meat would make some animals sick. But the harpy eagle's digestive system can handle it.

Because of their larger size, females tend to go after larger prey. The smaller males tackle smaller animals but may hunt more often. This difference in hunting styles probably helps the birds survive. Together, the eagles have a greater variety of animals to eat.

GO DEEPER

MANY BIRDS EAT FRUIT OR BERRIES. IF A HARPY EAGLE WERE REALLY HUNGRY, WOULD IT EAT THESE FOODS? WHY OR WHY NOT?

The Harpy Eagle's Life

Like other birds, harpy eagles hatch from eggs. Long before the eggs are laid, a male and female begin building a nest. First, they find a good platform high in a tree. The perfect spot has to be large and stable, because the nest will be huge. It may be more than 5 feet (1.5 m) from side to side. It can also be more than 1 foot (0.3 m) deep.

Hundreds of carefully placed sticks and branches make up the nest. When a harpy finds a suitable branch, he will grab it with his toes. Clutching it, he will flap his wings until the branch snaps. Then it's off to the nest with his prize.

[21ST CENTURY SKILLS LIBRARY]

Before the nest is finished, the adults line it with soft materials. Tender, young leaves and shreds of animal fur complete the nest.

A harpy eagle nest needs to be very high up in a tree.

Once the nest is finished, the eagles mate. Soon afterward, the female lays one or two large eggs. For the next 8 weeks, she spends most of her time warming the eggs. Her mate brings her food and occasionally takes his turn sitting on the eggs.

In time, a chick begins to peck its way out of the egg. This process may take a while. But eventually, the chick **emerges** from its shell and flops out into the nest. At this point, the mother stops warming the other egg. This egg never hatches.

Actually, the second egg is a "backup." If one egg fails to hatch, the parents still have a chick from the other egg. Losing one egg is a survival tactic. Young eagles demand lots of care and attention. It would be almost impossible for the parents to raise two growing eagles. So they produce one egg and a spare. Then they focus their attention on the chick that hatches.

A harpy eagle mother waits for one of her eggs to hatch.

A harpy chick has a black beak, oversized feet, and downy white feathers. For its first few months, it relies completely on its parents for food. The adults take turns catching prey and bringing it home. Inside the nest, they tear off shreds of meat to feed their young one. Meantime, the chick learns to stand and walk around the nest. It stretches and flaps its little wings. It sheds its soft downy feathers, replacing them with sturdier ones.

At about 6 months, the young eagle takes its first flight. This short flight gives it a chance to try taking off, steering, and landing. Even after it becomes an expert, it does not fly far from the nest. For many months, it continues to return home and beg for food.

This harpy eagle chick is 4 months old.

When the eagle is 5 or 6 years old, it is ready to find a mate. Once they build their first nest together, the pair may use it for years. Each year, they spruce it up by adding new sticks and lining it with fresh, soft materials. Every other year, they will mate and raise a chick. Pairs of harpies stay together for life, which can be 30 years or more.

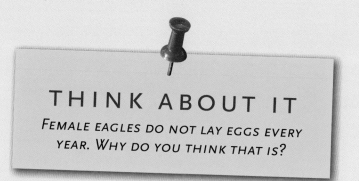

THINK ABOUT IT

FEMALE EAGLES DO NOT LAY EGGS EVERY YEAR. WHY DO YOU THINK THAT IS?

PROBLEMS FOR THE HARPIES

Harpy eagles are apex predators. In their natural **habitat**, they are fairly safe from harm. But in recent years, harpies have become less safe. There are two main reasons for this. People sometimes shoot them, and the harpies' natural habitat is shrinking.

Why would someone shoot these magnificent birds? Sometimes families who live near the rainforest might be worried that harpy eagles will attack their children, farm animals, or pets. Still other people shoot them just to show off or because they want to see the birds up close.

Shrinking habitat is another problem. Forests are being destroyed in Mexico and in Central and South

Harpy eagles are fierce enough that no other animal wants to mess with them, but humans are still a threat.

America. Logging companies have set up mills just outside the rainforest. There, workers turn trees into lumber for furniture or flooring. They process wood into pulp for making paper.

The harpy eagles need large forested areas to survive. A pair of eagles will rule a **territory** the size of a small town. They nest in rainforest trees that are twice as tall as oak trees. They drive out other harpies that move in too close. As more and more trees fall, the harpy eagles simply cannot find food, mates, or nesting places.

Fortunately, many people are working to solve this problem. One international group is keeping track of the harpy eagle population. It says that the harpy eagle numbers are decreasing. However, the birds are not yet in danger of becoming extinct. Another group is educating people about harpies. They want everyone to understand that eagles do not attack children. Other groups are urging people not to buy products made from rainforest lumber.

The harpy eagle population isn't endangered, but if people keep killing them, they may be someday.

In some places, the situation may be turning around. Native people who live in the rainforest have learned to protect the eagles' nests. Education programs are helping more people to understand the importance of predators.

In 2008, scientists spotted a pair of nesting eagles in a forest in Belize. It had been 50 years since harpies had been seen in this Central American country. Perhaps this nesting pair is a sign that the work is paying off.

By clearing away trees in harpy eagle territory, people are taking away the eagles' places to build nests.

LOOK AGAIN

HERE ARE SOME OF THE RAINFOREST TREES. WHAT MAKES THEM ESPECIALLY ATTRACTIVE TO LOGGERS?

THINK ABOUT IT

- Chapter 1 tells of a harpy eagle grabbing a lizard. These eagles usually kill their prey very quickly. Why is it better to fly off carrying dead prey instead of live prey?

- Apex predators, like harpy eagles, are at the top of the food chain. Go online or visit the library to find examples of other apex predators that live in the rainforest.

- Chapter 5 has some solutions for keeping the harpy eagle safe. If you were trying to help the eagles, what would you do?

LEARN MORE

FURTHER READING

Nguyen, Nam, and Sarah Hines Stephens. *Extreme Rainforest*. New York: Kingfisher Books, 2011.

Parry-Jones, Jemima. *Eagle & Birds of Prey*. New York: DK Children, 2000.

Spelman, Lucy. *National Geographic Animal Encyclopedia: 2,500 Animals with Photos, Maps, and More!* Washington DC: National Geographic Children's Books, 2012.

WEB SITES

Kids.Monagbay—Harpy Eagle
http://kids.mongabay.com/animal-profiles/harpy-eagle.html
Visit this site for more information, close-up photos, and links to pages about other rainforest animals.

PBS Nature—Jungle Eagle
http://www.pbs.org/wnet/nature/episodes/jungle-eagle/full-episode/7324/
Watch as a wildlife filmmaker studies a harpy eagle's rainforest nest, a chick, and the interactions between chick and parent.

San Diego Zoo Kids—Harpy Eagle
http://kids.sandiegozoo.org/animals/birds/harpy-eagle
The San Diego Zoo's site gives facts about the harpy eagle and has an audio button so that you can hear the eagles.

GLOSSARY

apex (AY-pex) at the very top

canopy (KAN-uh-pee) cover formed by the leafy upper branches in a forest

emerges (ih-MURJ-ez) comes out from a hidden place

habitat (HAB-ih-tat) place where a plant or animal naturally lives

mammals (MAM-uhlz) animals that have hair or fur and that produce milk for their young

peccaries (PEK-uh-reez) piglike mammals with hooves

talon (TAL-uhn) the sharp claw of a bird

territory (TER-i-tor-ee) an area that an animal inhabits and defends

INDEX

[21ST CENTURY SKILLS LIBRARY]